Better Homes and Gardens®

Crafts
FOR LITTLE KIDS

101
really,
really, really
fun ideas!

Better Homes
and Gardens® Books
Des Moines, Iowa

Crafts
FOR LITTLE KIDS

Better Homes and Gardens® Books
An imprint of Meredith® Books

Editor: Carol Field Dahlstrom
Writer: Susan M. Banker
Graphic Designer: Angela Haupert Hoogensen
Craft Project Assistant: Judy Bailey
Copy Chief: Terri Fredrickson
Copy and Production Editor: Victoria Forlini
Editorial Operations Manager: Karen Schirm
Managers, Book Production: Pam Kvitne,
  Marjorie J. Schenkelberg
Contributing Copy Editor: Arianna McKinney
Contributing Proofreaders: Karen Grossman,
  Colleen Johnson, Sheila Mauck
Photographers: Andy Lyons Cameraworks,
  Peter Krumhardt, Scott Little
Technical Illustrator: Chris Neubauer Graphics, Inc.
Electronic Production Coordinator: Paula Forest
Editorial and Design Assistants: Kaye Chabot,
  Mary Lee Gavin, Karen McFadden

Meredith® Books
Editor in Chief: Linda Raglan Cunningham
Design Director: Matt Strelecki
Executive Editor, Food and Crafts: Jennifer Dorland Darling

Publisher: James D. Blume
Executive Director, Marketing: Jeffrey Myers
Executive Director, New Business Development:
  Todd M. Davis
Executive Director, Sales: Ken Zagor
Director, Operations: George A. Susral
Director, Production: Douglas M. Johnston
Business Director: Jim Leonard

Vice President and General Manager: Douglas J. Guendel

***Better Homes and Gardens*® Magazine**
Editor in Chief: Karol DeWulf Nickell

Meredith Publishing Group
President, Publishing Group: Stephen M. Lacy
Vice President-Publishing Director: Bob Mate

Meredith Corporation
Chairman and Chief Executive Officer: William T. Kerr

Chairman of the Executive Committee: E. T. Meredith III

All of us at Better Homes and Gardens® Books are
dedicated to providing you with information and ideas to
create beautiful and useful projects. We welcome your
comments and suggestions. Write to us at: Better Homes
and Gardens Books, Crafts Editorial Department, 1716
Locust Street—LN112, Des Moines, IA 50309-3023.

If you would like to purchase any of our crafts, cooking,
gardening, home improvement, or home decorating and
design books, check wherever quality books are sold. Or
visit us at: bhgbooks.com

Cover Photography: Andy Lyons

it's all about the kids!

When we started this book of Crafts for Little Kids, we knew it would be fun. But who knew we would share such energy, enthusiasm, and excitement with a host of such talented little artists? Whether they were just three years old or the ripe old age of eight, these kids loved to create! We could hardly get them to stop painting, drawing, cutting, coloring, or gluing long enough to take photos of them working!

The real beauty of watching these little ones create was that they loved making and doing the projects rather than worrying about how the end product would look. The art of creation was the joy that they found, and the giggles and smiles we saw were just what we had hoped for. All of the fun-to-make projects in this book are kid tested, and the kids loved each and every one of these works of art. These children saw things with a fresh and excited eye, picked color combinations that sparkled, and painted and drew images that only a young mind could create. Look for a special kid-tested stamp beside these projects in the book.

So settle down with your little ones and join in the fun of making these magical projects—creations that begin in the minds of young children and end with the smiles of the lucky ones around them.

Carol Field Dahlstrom

How to use the book

Have you ever sat back and watched a child, deep in thought, with crayons and paper in hand? The creations that follow are nothing less than precious. What fun for kids to express themselves artistically, with the freedom to design whatever comes to mind! It's no secret that kids love to create. Whether you supply them with pipe cleaners or a paintbrush, colored paper or feathers, kids smile with anticipation as they start to form their next creations.

The inspiring projects in this book are geared to suit little Picassos ages three to eight. And each of the projects has been kid tested, so we know they are as doable as they are irresistible! (No kidding, moms tell us they had to pry some kids away from their supplies at bedtime!)

KID TESTED

Included with each project are a list of materials and step-by-step instructions to help you guide your child along. We've worked hard to include terminology that the kids will understand and have broken down the steps to make the crafting process as easy as possible. After all, we want smiles of success!

In the few instances where a sharp tool is used, we've indicated that the child needs the

4

Kids love to create, and now you can help them explore their creative side with wonderful projects guiding the way.

assistance of a grown-up (that's you!).

Also, if any steps are a bit tricky, we've asked for adult help. Once you show children how, they'll be proud to do it all by themselves (a very popular thing among little munchkins, we have discovered!).

The projects in this book cover a wide variety of techniques, from painting with sponges to painting with feet. Your kids are bound to discover some new methods that they'll want to try over and over again. Our hope is that this book provides fun-to-do projects that not only teach kids something, but also inspire them to explore their own creativity, increasing their knowledge as well as their interest in crafts.

Thank you for purchasing this book for your kids and for encouraging creativity in young minds. Together you're sure to create keepsakes that will be treasured for years to come!

Table of contents

4 Make Some Holiday Fun

Show your creativity around the house all year long with wonderful projects that celebrate the holidays! From Christmas trims you'll want to keep forever to polka-dot eggs the Easter Bunny would be proud to share, you'll find dozens of clever projects to brighten the seasons.

PAGES 72-99

5 Craft With Your Best Friend

There's nothing like spending time with a best friend to bring a smile to your face. This chummy chapter of crafts includes projects you can make with your buddies—even some things you can make to give as special surprises. From pet dishes to dress-up purses, you'll find new ways to share friendship.

PAGES 100-111

6 Use Your Big Imagination

Roll up your sleeves and get ready to paint macaroni, shape beads with clay, and print writing paper using toy cars! This supercreative chapter is so fun that you'll want to make these projects again and again!

PAGES 112-141

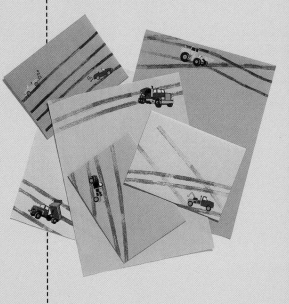

Colorful Bear Cave, by Laurel, age 3

choose colors that you know

Pick your favorite colors to make the cool projects in this chapter! Paint a fence with a brush or print a plastic container with your fingers. Try making a necklace that's as pretty as a rainbow or wrap a vase in shiny string. From crayon-colored pinwheels to foam-shape daisies in decorated flowerpots, you'll enjoy oodles of fun crafts projects using COLOR!

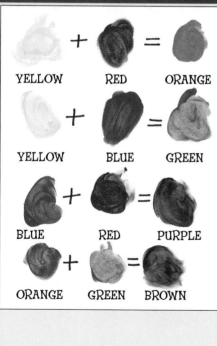

YELLOW	+	RED	=	ORANGE
YELLOW	+	BLUE	=	GREEN
BLUE	+	RED	=	PURPLE
ORANGE	+	GREEN	=	BROWN

KID
TESTED

Spinning tops

Twirl these little wood tops off your fingertips and see what your painted designs look like when the colors spin and appear to blend together!

what you'll need

Short lengths of
   ¹/₄-inch wood dowels
Wood disks or wheels
   (find them at
   crafts stores)
Saw (for grown-up
   use only!)
Pencil sharpener
Acrylic paint
Paintbrushes
Jewels
Thick white
   crafts glue

here's how

1 Let a grown-up cut dowels to fit through disks or wheels, leaving about 1 inch on each side of the disk.

2 Sharpen the dowel in a pencil sharpener. Put it in the hole of the disk.

3 Paint the top all one color. Pick another color to decorate the top so when it spins, it will make a new color. Paint dots, stripes, or other patterns. Look at the chart on the opposite page to see what the colors make when mixed together. Let dry. Glue a jewel to the flat end of the dowel. Let dry. Spin the top to see what new colors the spinning top makes.

Creativity fence

what you'll need

Bright outdoor latex
   paints in desired
   colors, such as
   white, green, yellow,
   pink, lavender, red,
   and blue
White picket fence
   (find it at
   home centers)
Old clothes and shoes
Paintbrushes
Disposable plate
Sponges, including a
   round stamping
   sponge with handle

here's how

1 When blending colors
   for a fence, choose
   colors that look bright
   and pretty when
   mixed together. On
this fence, the kids
used aqua, lime green,
lavender, pink, yellow,
and orange.

2 Begin with a clean,
   dry fence and
wear old clothes
and shoes. Blend two
or three colors
together on one piece
of wood. Use a
different brush for
each color. Use a clean
paintbrush to blend
the colors together.
Do this until the
fence piece is
completely painted.
Let it dry.

3 Pour a little bit of
   white paint onto a
disposable plate.

continued on page 14

Mixing and blending just the right colors together
   make very pretty fencing. Use pure colors
and your fence will look bright and cheery!

Holding the handle, dip the sponge into the paint and press onto the fence.

4 Sponge round shapes in circles to make flowers. Let the paint dry. Sponge yellow circles in the centers of the flowers.

Let the paint dry. Paint green stems and leaves. Let the paint dry.

Newspapers
Wood spools and/or
    small spools with
    thread on them
Black acrylic paint
Paintbrush
Wood beads
Paint markers
Colored string
Scissors
Colored plastic beads
    in a variety of shapes

Nifty necklaces

here's how

1 Cover the work surface with newspapers. Paint the wood spools black, leaving one end unpainted. Set the spool on the unpainted end until dry. Turn the spool over and paint the end. Let it dry. Paint the wood beads black.

2 Using paint markers, draw dots or other simple designs on the black spools. Let dry.

3 Cut a piece of string large enough for a necklace, adding about 4 inches for tying. Thread onto the string the painted beads, plastic beads, painted spools and/or spools with thread in the order you want. When the string is almost full, knot the ends together. Cut off the extra string.

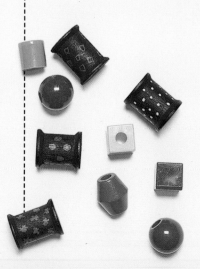

16

Make a pretty necklace to wear with your
favorite clothes. You pick the colors, then get busy painting
and stringing your cool spool beads!

Color-mixing magic

Whether you use frosting or paint, mixing colors is magic!
This two-part project teaches you what colors do when
painting a container or frosting crackers.

18

what you'll need to make the containers

Acrylic paints in red, yellow, blue, and white
Small disposable plates
Colored take-out containers (find them at party supply stores)

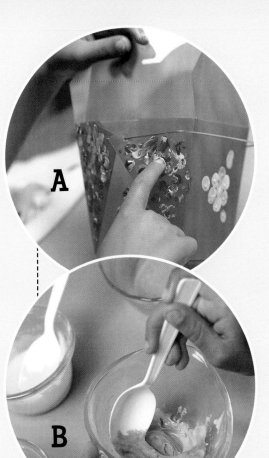

A

here's how

1 Using fingers, mix paint on a plate. Test mixing different colors together to see what new colors they make. Dip a finger in paint and dab a design on the container as shown in Photo A, right. Let dry.

KID TESTED

My Flower Garden, by Evelyn, age 5

what you'll need to mix the frosting

Medium-size bowl
Spoons
2 cups powdered sugar
1/4 cup milk
Small bowls
Food coloring in red, yellow, and blue
Graham crackers

B

here's how

1 In a bowl mix together powdered sugar and milk to make frosting.

2 Divide the frosting into three parts. Using food coloring, make one part red, one blue, and one yellow.

3 Using empty bowls, mix a little of two colors of frosting as shown in Photo B. What color did you get? Spread frosting on each cracker. Place the frosted crackers in the container or eat!

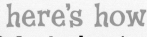

Recycle plastic and glass bottles by turning them into snazzy vases! Wind embroidery floss carefully around a bottle to make stripes, or wrap it unevenly to create a vase that is loaded with color and texture.

what You'll need

Glass or plastic bottle
Thick white crafts glue
Embroidery floss

here's how

1 Wash the bottle. Let it dry.

2 Place a dot of glue at the bottom edge of the bottle. Begin wrapping the embroidery floss around the bottle, keeping the wraps close together and adding more dots of glue when needed.

3 When you want to change colors, cut the floss and glue the end in place.

4 Continue making stripes of color like this until the entire bottle is covered with floss. Let the glue dry.

KID TESTED

Water and Sky Vase, by Ryan, age 8

20

Color-wrapped Vases

Dot game

Turn these colorfully painted wood disks
upside down and you're ready to enjoy a
friendly game of matchup!

what you'll need

20 wood disks about 1½ inches wide (find them with the wood supplies at crafts stores)
5 colors of acrylic paints plus black; paintbrush
Pencil with eraser
Round cardboard box

here's how

1 Separate the disks into five groups of four. Paint one side of the disks in each group a solid color. Use a different color for each group, such as four orange, four purple, four red, four teal, and four lime green. Let dry.

2 Paint dots onto the painted side of the disks. To paint the dots, dip the pencil eraser in paint and dot onto the painted disk. Let dry. Paint two of each disk color exactly the same. Put from one to eight dots on each disk. Make sure that each disk has a match.

3 On three pairs of disks, paint the dots with two colors like we did on the lime green, purple, and orange disks (they have four dots, five dots, and seven dots).

4 Paint the edges and back sides of each disk black. Let dry.

5 To decorate a box to hold the disks, paint it black. Let it dry. Paint different colored dots on the box.

6 To play the dot game: On a flat surface, turn all of the disks over so the dots are facedown. Mix up

the disks. Place the mixed-up disks in rows. Taking turns, turn over only two disks at a time in search of a match. If they match, keep them in front of you in a pile and take another turn. If the disks do not match, place them dot-side down in the same places you took them from. Continue taking turns until all the disks are gone. The person with the most disks at the end of the game is the winner!

Color-it-pretty pinwheels

Pick out all your best-loved colors from your crayon box and use them on paper! After you color a sheet, turn it into an awesome blow-in-the-wind pinwheel!

what you'll need

Ruler; paper; pencil
Crayons, colored pencils, or marking pens; scissors; dime
Crafting foam star cutout; large beads
Straight pin with large plastic head
Pencil with eraser
Eraser from the end of a pencil

here's how

1 With a pencil and ruler, mark an 8$\frac{1}{2}$-inch square on the back side of the paper. Color the paper on both sides as you wish. Cut out the square.

2 Draw pencil lines from corner to corner on the back of the paper to make an X as shown below. Place the dime in the center, where the + is, on the back of the paper and draw around it.

3 Using scissors, cut along each line of the X, being careful to cut only up to the circle you drew around the dime.

4 Draw a star about the size of a dime on foam and cut it out. Place a bead and the foam star on the pin.

5 Without folding, bend every other point to the center of the square. Have a grown-up help push the pin through all four points of the pinwheel, one at a time, and then through the center of the square.

6 Place a bead onto the pin behind the pinwheel. Push the pin through the pencil eraser. Push an eraser onto the end of pin as shown in the assembly diagram, right, to secure and cover the pin tip.

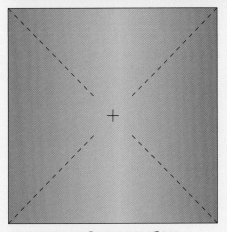

PINWHEEL-MARKING DIAGRAM

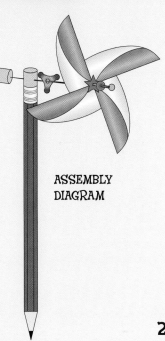

ASSEMBLY DIAGRAM

Pom-pom pretties

Like colors on a color wheel, this hat and scarf set is splashed with all the colors of a rainbow.

what You'll need

Plastic bag
Felt beret-style hat
Felt scarf
Assorted sizes of pom-poms
Fabric glue

here's how

1 Tuck a plastic bag into the beret so that the glue will not soak through. Lay the beret and scarf on a flat surface.

2 Arrange pom-poms on beret. Put a large pom-pom in the center and smaller ones around the edge. Arrange the pom-poms in rows, group colors, or make any pattern you wish.

3 One at a time, remove the pom-poms, apply a large amount of fabric glue to each one, and press onto the hat where it was placed. Decorate the scarf in the same way. When one side of the scarf is done and dry, turn it over and do the other side. Let the glue dry.

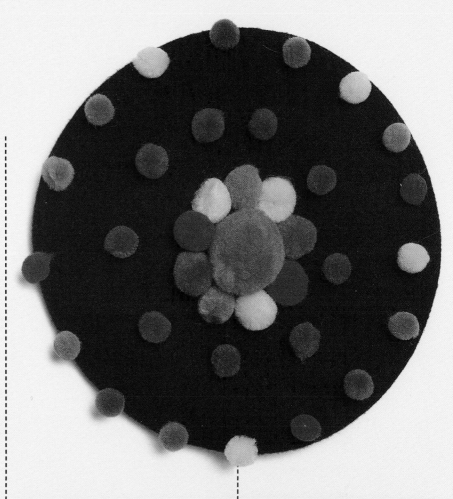

USE YOUR IMAGINATION!

What else could you use to decorate a hat and scarf set (or the cuffs of gloves or mittens)? Here are some ideas to get you thinking:
⇒ Buttons
⇒ Appliqués (those cutouts in the sewing area of crafts, discount, and fabric stores)
⇒ Satin flowers
⇒ Rhinestones

⇒ Small doll accessories (such as shoes, purses, and gloves)

TIP: If you use something other than pom-poms to decorate your winter clothes, use the right kind of glue. Have a grown-up read the glue label with you to be sure what you glue on will stay put when you go out to play!

what you'll need

Terra-cotta flowerpot
Dirt; seeds or a small plant
Wide green crafts stick
Black permanent marking pen
Sticky-back crafting foam flowers and circles

here's how

1 Fill the terra-cotta pot with dirt. Plant seeds or a small plant in dirt.

2 Use a marking pen to write your name on the crafts stick, leaving at least 1 1/2 inches blank on each end. Push one end of the stick into the center of the flowerpot.

3 Decide where you want to put foam flowers on the flowerpot. Layer the pieces if you want to make colorful flowers. Peel off the backing and press into place. Press on foam dots if you wish. Make a large foam flower and press it onto the top of the crafts stick.

Fancy flowerpots

Make a cheery decoration that is as colorful as a flower from the garden. Peel-and-stick foam pieces make it easy to grow these pretty blooms.

My Fingers and Toes, by Olivia, age 4

use your hands and feet

Get creative with paint—you'll be surprised at all the neat stuff you can make with hands, feet, and fingers! Plus we'll show you how to decorate some adorable summer flip-flops, dinnertime dot-to-dots, and glassware that will brighten up any meal of the day. Using your hands and feet has never been such a treat!

Feel like a princess at the beach or at the pool with these fancy sandals on your feet.

Beach flip-flops

what you'll need

Solid-color flip-flop-style sandals
Bright pink acrylic enamel paint
Paintbrush
White sparkle yarn
Ruler; scissors
Crafts glue
$3/4$-inch-wide sheer white ribbon
Bright pink metallic curling ribbon

here's how

1 Paint vertical stripes (up and down) on the edge of each flip-flop. Let the paint dry.

2 Cut two 24-inch-long pieces of yarn. Glue one end of the yarn to the underside of the plastic strap where it meets the bottom of the sandal. Wrap the entire strap with yarn. Trim away the extra yarn. Glue yarn end to back side of plastic strap. Let dry. Repeat for the other flip-flop.

3 Tie a small ribbon bow for each flip-flop. Use curling ribbon to tie a bow to the top of each flip-flop.

KID TESTED

Fancy Flip-Flops, by Clarissa, age 5

USE YOUR IMAGINATION!

Personalize your flip-flops by tying something special to each bow. Here are some ideas to get you started:
⇒ Plastic butterflies
⇒ Silver or gold charms
⇒ Buttons
⇒ Plastic fashion rings
⇒ Silk flowers
⇒ Large beads
⇒ Game pieces
⇒ Seashells

Turn your handprints into a lovely bouquet. Pick your very favorite colors to make the daisylike blooms on an apron.

All-abloom apron

what you'll need

Newspapers

White apron (Find it at kitchen supply stores. A tighter weave takes the print easier.)

Cotton fabric or paper scraps

Fabric paints (acrylics used with textile medium can be used instead but will leave a harder textured print)

$1/2$-inch-wide paintbrush

here's how

1. Cover a flat work surface with newspapers. Lay the apron top on the newspapers. Use cotton fabric or paper scraps for practice prints.

2. Ask a grown-up to use a $1/2$-inch paintbrush to spread paint evenly over your outstretched hand.

3. Have a grown-up help position your hand paint-side down with fingers stretched apart over the apron top. Gently press your hand down onto the fabric. Work quickly so the paint doesn't dry before printing. Let the paint dry.

4. Wash your hands with soapy water. Dry your hands.

5. Use your finger to paint flower petals and small green leaves around the fingertips of your handprints.

Dot-to-dots are always great, and this extra big version makes eating time even more fun! Use the flower or sailboat patterns, or make your own playful design.

Dot-to-dot place mats

what You'll need

Tempera paint
Disposable plate
Paintbrush
Large pieces of butcher or white shelf paper
Place mat for pattern
Tissue paper; pencil
Scissors; black fine-line marking pen
Gift wrap to color coordinate; glue
Clear self-stick shelf liner
Pinking shears; crayon

here's how

1. Pour paint into a plate and spread with a brush. Ask a grown-up to help you place your hand, palm-side down, into paint. Rub hands together to put paint on other hand.

2. Place hands onto white paper and press. Get more paint on hands. Leaving some white areas showing on the paper, continue making handprints. Print as many pieces of paper as you wish.

3. Trace around a place mat on a piece of tissue paper to make a pattern. Cut out the pattern and place over the printed paper. Trace around pattern and cut the place mat from the printed paper.

4. For the dot-to-dot pattern, look at page 39 for ideas. Trace a dot-to-dot pattern onto tissue paper. Lay the tissue paper over the handprint place mat and mark dots with pencil, poking holes in tissue paper with pencil point.

5. Make paint dots over the pencil dots using your finger.

6. Use a black marking pen to number the dots. Wait to connect the dots until finished.

continued on page 38

7 Cut long strips of gift wrap to fold around the edge of the place mat. Glue in place. Cut a backing from wrapping paper and glue to the back of the place mat.

8 Cut two pieces of clear self-stick plastic slightly larger than place mat. Have a grown-up help peel one-fourth of the backing off one piece and place sticky-side down over one end of the place mat. Smooth with your hands and slowly peel off more of the backing, smoothing clear self-stick plastic over place mat.

9 Repeat with the second piece of clear self-stick plastic on opposite side of place mat. Use pinking shears to trim away excess plastic.

10 Starting with number one and following the numbers in order, use a crayon to connect the dots on top of the clear plastic. Use a paper towel to wipe off the crayon for the next use.

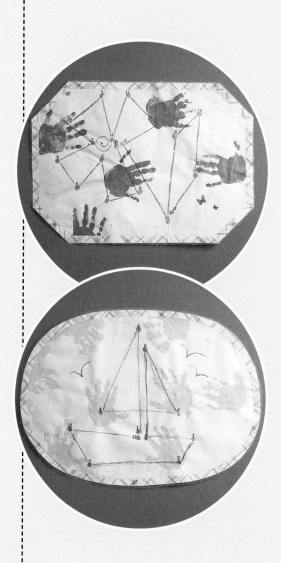

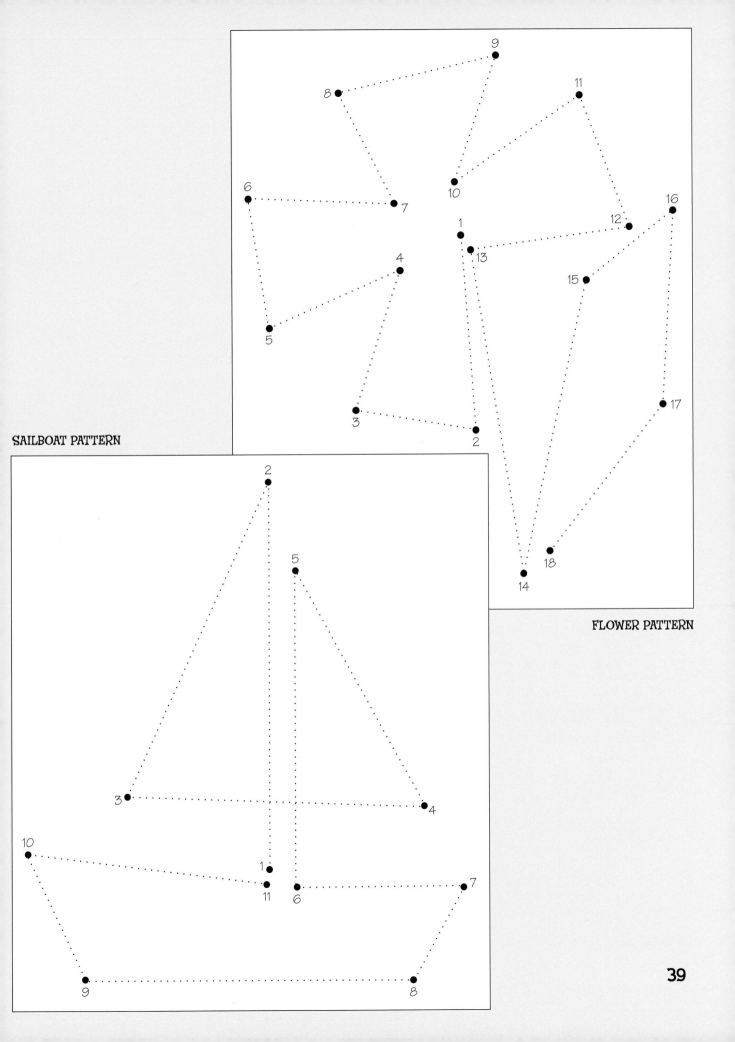

SAILBOAT PATTERN

FLOWER PATTERN

39

Fingerprint frame

Give your personal touch to picture mats by making itty-bitty fingerprint bugs with paint. Create ladybugs, caterpillars, and butterflies with black marking pen details or make any creepy-crawly critters you like!

what you'll need

Acrylic paints in good bug colors

Frame with double mats

Black fine-line marking pen

here's how

1 To make ladybugs, dip a finger in red paint. Press finger onto one of the photo mats. Make as many red dots as you wish, leaving spaces between the dots. Let the paint dry. Draw dots and curly antennae with a marking pen.

2 To make caterpillars, dip a finger in green paint. Make a bunch of dots in an uneven line. Continue making lines of dots with your finger, leaving space between bugs. Let dry. Make faces and antennae with a marking pen.

3 To make butterflies, dip a finger in any color of paint and make two prints, side by side. Continue making butterfly wings like this until you like the way the mat looks. Let dry. Use a marking pen to add details, such as spots and antennae.

Rainbow Butterflies, by Ryan, age 8

KID TESTED

Roll up your sleeves and make painted fingerprints that leave your mark on dishes with one-of-a-kind designs.

what you'll need
No-bake glass or
 plastic paints
Disposable plate
Ceramic, glass, or
 plastic dishes
Plasticware

Fingerprint dishes

here's how

Pour small dots of paint into a flat disposable plate. To make fingerprint designs, dip your finger into paint.

Avoiding the areas where the food will touch, dot and draw around the edge of a plate, the side and handle of a cup, or onto the handles of plasticware. Let the paint dry.

Red, Yellow, and Blue Dishes, opposite, by Olivia and Michaela, both age 5

Polka-Dot Dishes, left, by Clarissa, age 5

KID TESTED

Take off your shoes and socks, and have fun squashing paint between your toes! This fancy footwork will keep a clean footpath in your bedroom or playroom.

Walk-around rug

what you'll need

Acrylic paints in colors you like

Flat work trays, such as metal baking pans or cookie sheets

Paintbrush

Large pieces of paper

Cotton throw rug

here's how

1 Pour paint into flat trays and spread with a paintbrush.

2 If you would like, use paper and experiment with making your footprints in different ways. When you like how they look, make them on the rug.

3 To make a footprint flower, place your heel in one color of paint. Press your heel in the center of the rug. Wash your foot.

4 Place both feet in another color of paint. Place your feet around the flower center to make petals. Place your feet in paint again before adding more petals. Continue until you like the look of your flower.

5 To make designs on edges of rug, press just your toes into paint and place on rug, changing colors when you want to. Let the paint dry.

Friends' names look really neat—
especially when they're on your feet!
Invite your friends to write their names
on your shoes with colorful marking pens.

Autograph shoes

what you'll need

Purchased canvas
tennis shoes
Permanent marking
pens
Crafts glue
Colored jewels
Yarn in bright colors
Scissors

here's how

1 Have friends write
their names on
the tennis shoes
using permanent
marking pens.

2 Using crafts glue,
stick jewels around
the names and on
other parts of the
shoes. Let the glue dry.

3 Cut the yarn the
length of shoelaces.
Thread the yarn
through the shoe holes
and tie as shoelaces.

My Playground in the Field, by Grace, age 7

go outside and play

Fresh-air fun awaits when you make things to use and play with in the sunshine! Put on a paper hat and march to the beat of your own band, drink from a jeweled goblet and pretend you are royalty, or create rock bugs for great outside pets. Gobs of giggles await as you go outside and play with these wonderful projects!

Sluggy bugs

what you'll need

Rocks and pebbles of interesting shapes and sizes

Acrylic paints in bright colors and black; paintbrushes

Black marking pen

Thick white crafts glue

here's how

1 Gather together cool rocks in many sizes. Wash and dry the rocks.

2 Arrange the rocks to look like an animal or other creature that you like.

3 Paint the large background areas of the rocks first. Let the paint dry.

4 Paint polka dots or other designs on the background or paint small pebbles to glue on later.

5 Use a thin paintbrush to paint stripes. Let the paint dry.

6 To make the eyes, make some happy, sad, and angry. These eyes each use two pebbles, one for the center and one behind it. First paint the tiny pebbles black. Paint the slightly larger pebbles a light color or two colors if you want to make eyelids (like on the purple and yellow eyes, opposite). Let dry. Add details with black marking pen.

7 Glue the rocks and pebbles together or just lay the pieces together to make a creature. Let the glue dry.

Look at rocks in a whole new way! Use your wildest imagination to make lizards, turtles, aliens—whatever you can dream up!

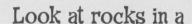

Dining with royalty

what you'll need for the goblets

Plastic goblets
Glitter paint; jewels

here's how

1. Wash the goblets. Let them dry.
2. Squirt a grape-size dot of glitter paint onto the goblet where you want each jewel. Press a jewel into the wet glitter paint as shown in Photo A, below. Let dry.

what you'll need for the king costume

Tracing paper; pencil
Scissors
Heavy gold paper
Stapler and staples
Self-adhesive fastener, such as Velcro

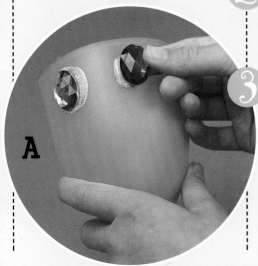

A

Serve your favorite drinks in jeweled goblets fit for any king or queen. Dress up for the party with these easy-to-make costumes.

Glitter glue; jewels
1¹/₃ yards glittery fabric
Safety pins
Fur trim

here's how

1. For the crown, trace the triangle shape, page 56, onto tracing paper, cut it out, and trace onto heavy gold paper six times. Cut out the triangles.
2. Overlap and staple the triangles together as shown on page 57 and above.
3. Try on the crown. Have a grown-up help you mark where to put fasteners so the crown fits you snugly. Have a grown-up help you stick the fasteners on each end.
4. Decorate the crown with jewels. Squirt a dot of glitter glue about the size of a pea where you want each jewel to be. Press the jewels into the glitter glue. Let them dry.
5. For the cape, have a grown-up help you cut a big circle from fabric. In the center, draw a small circle about the size of a small paper plate. Cut it out. Cut a slit to the center circle.
6. Use safety pins to attach the fur to the edges of the cape where you wish to have fur.

continued on page 54

what you'll need for the queen costume

Pencil
Heavy paper
Scissors; tape
Glitter paint
Pipe cleaners
Two 45-inch squares of
sheer fabric

here's how

1 To make the hat, use the hat measurements, opposite, as a guide. Have a grown-up draw the hat shape on paper. Cut out the shape.

2 Roll the paper into a cone and tape it together. Trim off the bottom edge with scissors to make a neat edge.

3 Decorate the hat with glitter paint and let it dry.

4 Using pipe cleaners, poke a hole on each side of hat. Twist pipe cleaners at the end to secure for a tie. Pull a corner of one piece of sheer fabric through the tip of hat and tape on the inside.

5 To make the gown, use the other piece of fabric. Take two corners that are beside each other and tie them together. Put on the gown with the tie over one shoulder.

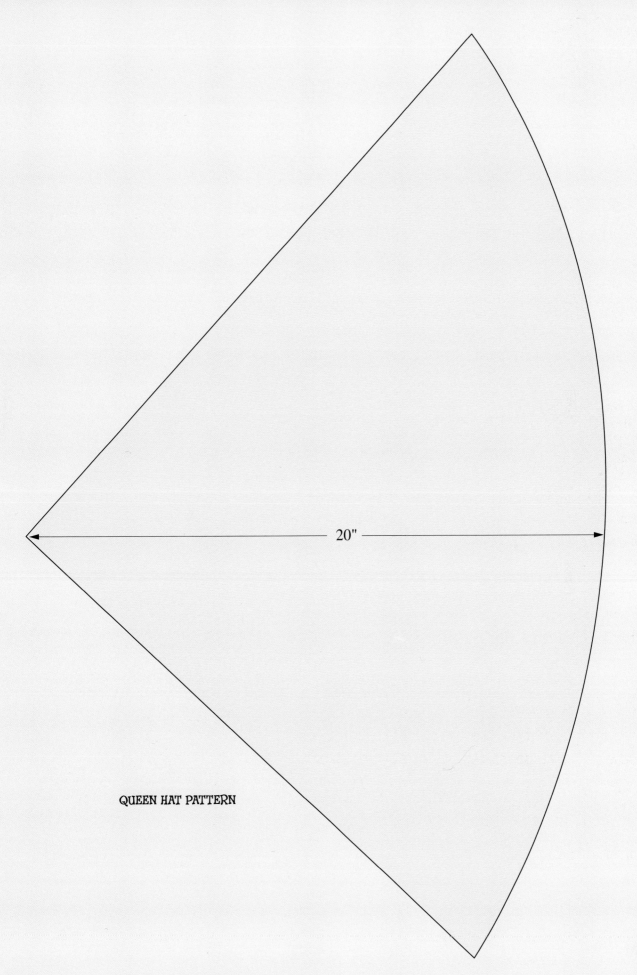

20"

QUEEN HAT PATTERN

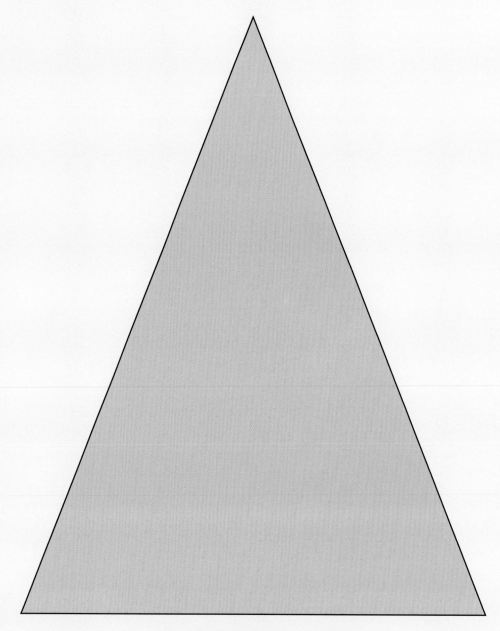

KING CROWN TRIANGLE PATTERN

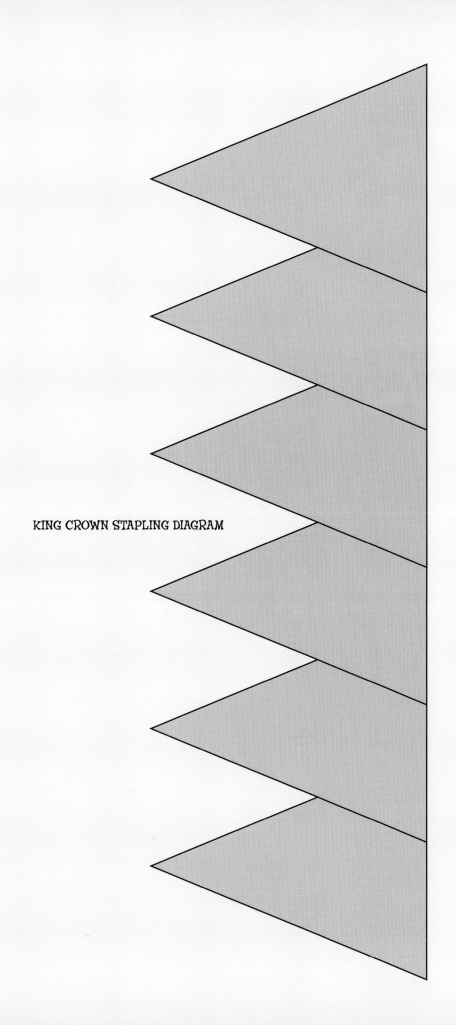

KING CROWN STAPLING DIAGRAM

High-flyin' flags

what you'll need

Rectangle of nylon fabric (find at fabric stores)
Water; acrylic paints; disposable plates; wide paintbrushes
Tracing paper; pencil; scissors; sponges
Colored paint markers; stick; colored duct tape

here's how

1 Decide on the design for the flag, looking at these two pages and the patterns on pages 60-61 for ideas. Lay the fabric on a work surface. Spray the fabric with water until it is wet.

2 Put a little of each paint color on a different plate. Mix with a little bit of water until the paints are runny. Paint the background colors using a wide paintbrush. Blend the colors together some if you want to. Let dry.

3 Trace the desired shapes for sponges from pages 60-61 onto tracing paper. Cut out the shapes. Trace around the patterns on sponges. Have a grown-up help cut out the sponge shapes.

4 Spread the paint color for stamping onto a plate. Soak the sponges in water and squeeze out the extra water. Dip a sponge in paint and stamp onto the fabric. Let dry.

5 Outline the shapes with colored paint markers. Let dry.

6 Paint the stick as you wish. Let dry. Lay flag on a table. Press tape around the flag edges. Tape the flag to the stick.

KID TESTED

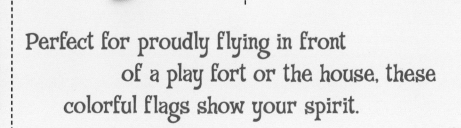

King Con's Flag,
by Con, age 6

Perfect for proudly flying in front of a play fort or the house, these colorful flags show your spirit.

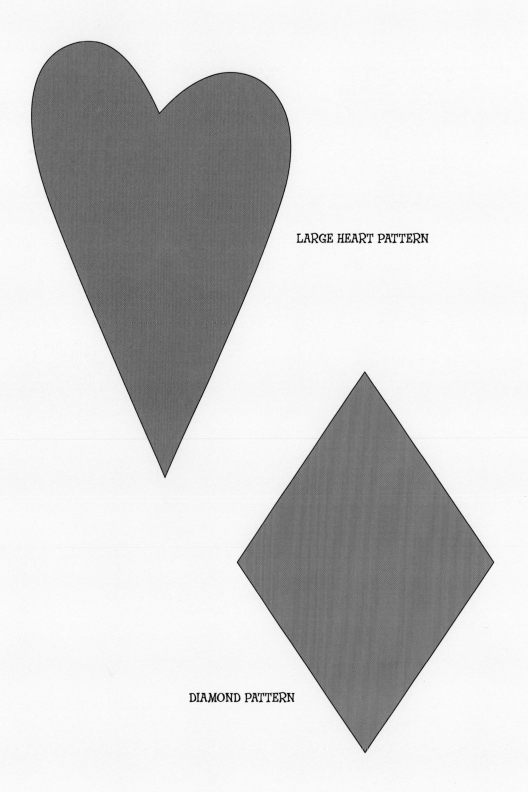

LARGE HEART PATTERN

DIAMOND PATTERN

60

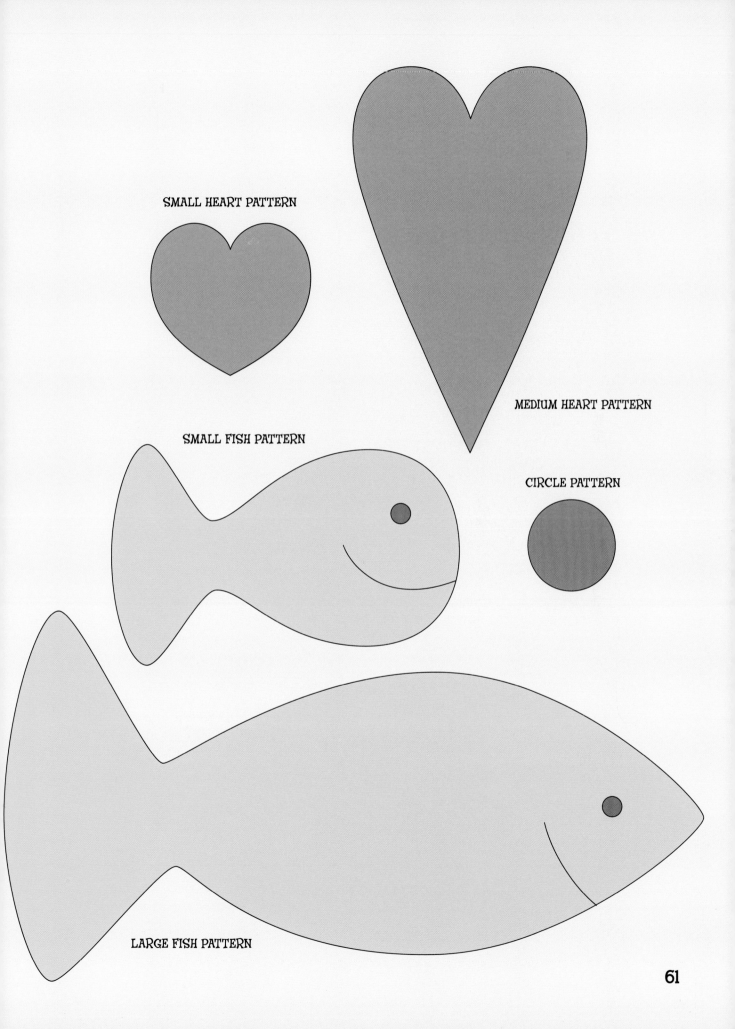

SMALL HEART PATTERN

MEDIUM HEART PATTERN

SMALL FISH PATTERN

CIRCLE PATTERN

LARGE FISH PATTERN

Make some music with
these playful instruments—
and wear your
paper hat and feather!

what you'll need for the hat
18×20-inch colored
    paper
Pinking shears
Feather

Marching band fun

here's how

1 Trim the short ends of the paper using pinking shears.

2 Using the diagrams, right, fold the paper to make a hat. Tuck a feather into the brim on one side.

continued on page 64

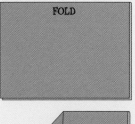
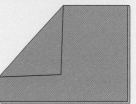
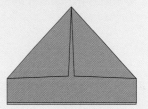
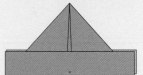

FOLD

HAT-FOLDING DIAGRAMS

Rat-a-tat drum

what you'll need for the drum

Round cardboard
   container, such as an
   oatmeal box
Utility knife (for
   grown-up use only!)
Colored paper; scissors
Glue stick
Large balloon; tape
Wide rickrack
Thick white crafts glue
Colored tacks
Colored cord
1-inch-wide
   ribbon

here's how

1 Using a clean and dry cardboard container, have a grown-up cut off the bottom with a utility knife.

2 Cut a piece of colored paper the same width as the container. Wrap the paper around the container and glue it in place.

3 Cut off the wide, round part of the balloon using scissors. Ask an adult to help stretch and pull the balloon over the top of the container. Tape the balloon all the way around the container.

4 Glue a piece of wide rickrack over the tape. Have a grown-up help you press about eight colored tacks around the outer edge of the container on each end. Press them only partway in, putting glue on each tack point.

5 Starting with one tack, tie colored cord around it and then press the tack in the rest of the way.

6 Wind the cord around each tack to make a zigzag pattern (back and forth).

7 Cut a piece of ribbon for a neck strap to hold drum. Tack each end of ribbon onto the drum using a small dab of glue. Let dry.

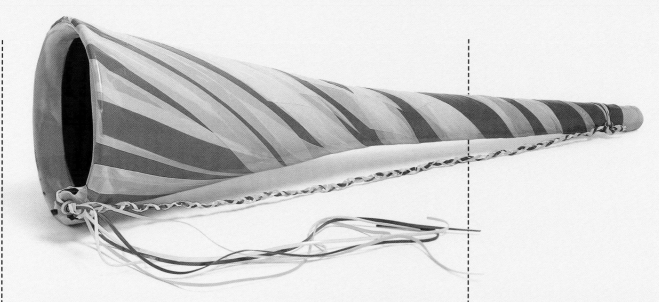

what you'll need for the trumpet

Long funnel with a tab and hole at wide end (find at discount stores)
Colored electrical tape
Scissors; plastic cord

here's how

1. Remove all stickers from the funnel. Wash and dry the funnel.

2. Starting at the narrow end, wrap the tape around the funnel until you reach the other end. Fold the tape over the edge and into the inside. Cut off the extra tape.

3. Continue adding more tape, using whatever colors you want. Wrap the funnel in tape until it is all covered.

4. Cut three strands of plastic cord to make a strap. Braid the strap and tie to the tab with the hole. Tape the other end onto the narrow end of the funnel.

5. Wrap tape around the narrow end to make the end look neat and hold the cord in place. If you wish, wrap tape along the inside edge of the funnel.

Pretend you're playing in a big brass band with this striped trumpet that's actually a funnel underneath.

Toot toot trumpet

Tambourine time

what you'll need for the tambourine

2 foil pie pans in your favorite color

Toothpick; pipe cleaners

Jingle bells

Hard dried beans, rice, or other items to place inside pans for noise

Sticky-back foil papers (find at scrapbook stores)

Scissors

here's how

1 Place foil pie pans' edges together with the insides of pans facing. Have a grown-up help poke 8 to 12 holes around the outer edges with a toothpick. Poke holes through both layers.

2 Keeping the holes together, pull a pipe cleaner through the pair of pans. Loop it through the hole a couple of times to hold it firmly in place. String a jingle bell onto the pipe cleaner and wind the pipe cleaner around the edge of pan, lacing pipe cleaners through all the holes. Add bells wherever you wish. When you are about halfway around the pan, place a handful of dried beans or other filler inside of pans. Continue lacing the edge of the pans to completely trap the beans.

3 Cut triangular shapes from sticky-back papers. Stick the papers on the flat part of the pans to create a star pattern.

With beans on the inside and jingle bells around the outside, this tambourine will make you dance.

Ring-a-ding-ding! These chiming bells
are made from small flowerpots.

what you'll need
Small clay pots
Wood dowel to fit in hole in pot
Saw (for grown-up use only!); ruler
Acrylic paints in pretty colors
Paintbrush
Thick white crafts glue
Yarn or cord; scissors
Round wood bead about $1/2$ to $3/4$ inch in diameter

here's how

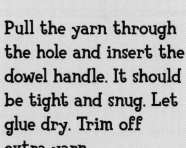

1 Choose several different sizes of clay pots if you wish. Different sizes make different sounds. Choose dowels that fit very snugly in the holes. Have an adult cut an 8-inch-long piece of dowel for each handle.

2 Paint the pots and dowels whatever colors you wish. Let the paint dry.

3 Place a dab of glue around the hole on the pot. Cut a piece of yarn 10 inches long. Tie the bead in a knot on one end of the yarn.

Pull the yarn through the hole and insert the dowel handle. It should be tight and snug. Let glue dry. Trim off extra yarn.

Clink-clank bells

You'll love to tend to the garden with this brightly decorated watering can.

what you'll need

Tracing paper; pencil; scissors
Sticky-back crafting foam sheets; watering can

here's how

1 To cut foam shapes to decorate the watering can, use the patterns, below, or create your own shapes. To use the patterns, trace them and cut out the shapes. Trace around the shapes on foam and cut out.

2 To layer shapes, cut the center shape smaller than the background shape.

3 Peel off the paper backing from the foam shape. Press onto the watering can. Press smaller shapes onto the larger shapes.

Color-splashed watering can

TRIM PATTERNS

what You'll need
Sunglasses
Acrylic enamel paints; small paintbrush

here's how

1 When choosing how to paint your glasses, look at the different parts of the frames. Paint each part a different color if you like.

2 If possible, take the lenses out of frames so they won't get painted. Paint the main color and let it dry. Paint it two or three times. Always make sure the paint is dry before applying another coat of paint.

3 When the main background color is dry, add stripes or dots in different colors. Use a tiny paintbrush to make stripes. Use the handle of the paintbrush to make dots. Let the paint dry.

Super-duper sunglasses

Make ordinary sunglasses really "sun-sational" by dashing and dotting bright paint on the rims.

Cool Shades, by Meredith, age 7

Sharing My Heart, by Finn, age 6

make some holiday fun

Gather your crafting supplies and spice up this year's holiday decorations with your own creative talents! This festive chapter is bright with year-round ideas. Deck the halls with merry Christmas trims or surprise the Easter Bunny with "egg-cellent" eggs. Choose a project, to make every season of the year happy, happy, happy!

Halloween pumpkins

what You'll need

Pumpkin; thick white crafts glue; glitter
Paintbrush; tracing paper; pencil; scissors
Crafting foam in colors you like
Paper punch; metallic pipe cleaners

here's how

1 To stick glitter to the pumpkin, use a paintbrush or your fingertip to create glue designs. Do two or three designs at a time and then sprinkle with two colors of glitter. Continue making glitter designs all over your pumpkin.

2 To make the foam decorations, trace the patterns you like on pages 76-77. Cut out the shapes. Trace around the shapes on foam. Cut out. Glue the pieces in place. Make glitter designs where you want to.

3 Using a paper punch, make a hole at the top of each foam piece. Push a pipe cleaner through each hole and twist to secure. Wrap the pipe cleaners around a pencil. Wrap the loose ends around the pumpkin stem.

KID TESTED

Afraidy Cat, by Morgan, age 4

These sparkling pumpkins shine among your jack-o'-lanterns—and they last longer too!

STAR PATTERNS

76

MOON PATTERN

PUMPKIN PATTERN

GHOST PATTERN

CAT PATTERN

77

These soft feather angels
are so heavenly to craft!
Make one to give to Mom or Dad!

KID TESTED

Angelica and Angie Angels, by Kourtni, age 8

Feather angels

here's how

1 Use scissors to cut off the tip of the cone.

2 Spread glue on half of the outside of the cone. Choose feathers that look pretty together. Place the feathers on the glue, facing all the feathers in the same direction with the wide ends pointing downward. When the first half is done, cover the other half of the cone with glue and feathers.

3 For wings, glue large feathers on the back.

4 Wrap one end of the pipe cleaner tightly around a pencil four times. Remove it from the pencil. Push the straight end of the pipe cleaner through the bead down to where it curls. Push the pipe cleaner into the tip of the cone and tape it in place on the inside of the cone.

what You'll need

Scissors
Paper cone cups (from bottled-water company)
White glue
Feathers; pipe cleaner
Pencil; large bead; tape

Merry macaroni ornaments

what You'll need

Pasta with holes in it
Disposable plate
Acrylic paints in your
    favorite colors
Paintbrushes
Beads
Pipe cleaners

here's how

1 Paint the pasta by placing it on a plate and painting many pieces at a time. Let the paint dry.

2 String beads and pasta onto the middle of the pipe cleaners. Leave a space at each end. Twist the ends together and form a hanger to place on the tree.

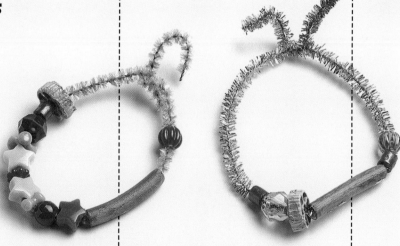

Christmas Rings, by Tess, age 3

Make pretty ornaments to put on your Christmas tree.
Just paint some macaroni and string some beads!

Pinecone pots

what You'll need

1¹/₂-inch terra-cotta flowerpots

Acrylic paints in pink, orange, purple, blue, green, yellow, and white; paintbrushes

Pinecones

Wood stars

Paper napkins

Thick white crafts glue

here's how

1 Paint the flowerpot a solid color. Let the paint dry.

2 Choose another color to make stripes or dots. To make stripes, use a tiny paintbrush. Rinse out the paint

Use your favorite color combinations to make a brilliant set of miniature trees to parade around your holiday home.

from the brush well before changing colors.

3 To make dots, dip the handle of a paintbrush into paint and dot onto the outside of the pot. Let dry.

4 Paint the pinecones white. Let dry. Paint them a second time if you need to so all the pinecone is white. Let the paint dry.

5 Paint the stars to match their pots, using the same paint colors. Let dry. Make little dots or stripes on the stars. Let dry.

6 Fill the pot with a piece of crumpled paper napkin if the pinecone is too small. Then put a lot of glue on the crumpled napkin. Set the pinecone onto the wet napkin and glue the star onto the pinecone.

KID TESTED

My Tiny Tree, by Jacob, age 7

what you'll need

Cardboard tube from toilet paper or paper towels
Colored paper
Pencil; ruler; scissors; glue stick
Glitter paint
Round jar lid
Acrylic paint; paintbrush
Thick white crafts glue
Beads and jewels
Orange or yellow feather

KID TESTED

Christmas Light, by Meredith, age 7

here's how

1. To make the colored paper the right size to cover the cardboard tube, lay the tube on the paper and draw a pencil line at the top of the tube. Roll the paper around the tube and mark another line where you need to cut it. Cut out the colored paper along the pencil lines.

2. Rub a glue stick over the back side of the paper and roll it around the tube.

3. Paint glitter paint along the top edge of candle. Glob on extra paint to make drips.

4. Paint the lid the color you wish. Let paint dry.

5. Use globs of glue to glue the candle into the bottom of the lid.

6. Put a lot of glitter paint into the lid around the candle and then press beads and jewels into the wet glitter.

7. Cut a point on the end of the feather to make it look like a flame. Glue the feather to the inside of the tube.

Feathers make a safe flame for these colorful Christmas candles that you decorate with glitter paint and jewels.

Feather candles

Winter Wonders

String up a clothesline full
of hats and mittens to welcome
your guests in out of the cold.

what You'll need

Crafting foam sheets or construction paper
Decorative-edge scissors; crafting foam cutouts
Small foam rollers 2 to 3 inches wide
Hot-glue gun; hot-glue sticks; tracing paper; pencil
Acrylic paints in colors you like
Disposable plates; paper towel
Pom-poms; straight scissors; string
Miniature clothespins

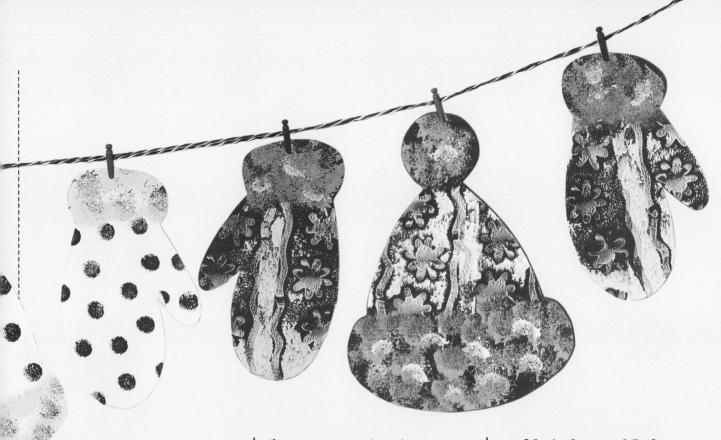

here's how

1 To make the rollers, cut foam strips with decorative-edge scissors. Have a grown-up help hot-glue them, along with the purchased cutouts, around the rollers.

2 Trace the mitten and hat patterns, pages 88–89, onto the foam or construction paper. Wait to cut out since they'll be easier to print in full sheets.

3 Print lighter colors on darker backgrounds and darker colors on lighter backgrounds.

Squeeze paint onto a disposable plate and roll the foam roller in the paint until the foam is completely covered. The trick to printing with a roller is to make a line without picking up the roller. Practice on blank paper before printing on the mitten

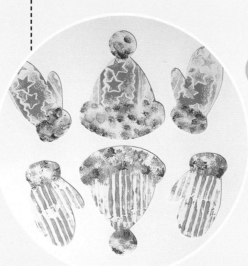

and hat shapes. Wash out the roller to switch colors and squeeze out extra water carefully with a paper towel.

4 Pinch the glitter pom-poms between your thumb and first finger, dip them into the paint, and then print them directly onto the hat and mittens. Let dry.

5 Cut out the hats and mittens. Use clothespins to hang them on a string clothesline.

HAT PATTERN

MITTEN PATTERN

Just a little clay and pretty jewels make the coolest
Valentines to give to someone you love so much.

Cards of clay

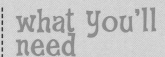

what You'll need

White air-dry clay, such as Crayola Model Magic
Rolling pin
Cookie cutter
Small beads and jewels
Textured red and white papers
Scissors
Thick white crafts glue

here's how

1. Use a rolling pin to flatten the white clay until it is about $1/4$ inch thick. Cut out a shape with a cookie cutter.

2. Before clay dries, press jewels or beads into the surface. Push them in firmly without smashing the clay.

3. Cut out shapes from textured papers. Glue the red and white papers together. Glue the clay shape on top.

I Love You Cards, by Clarissa, age 5, and Jack, age 7

Show your friends and family how much
you love them by making this sweet Valentine gift.
But be prepared for
some hugs and kisses in return!

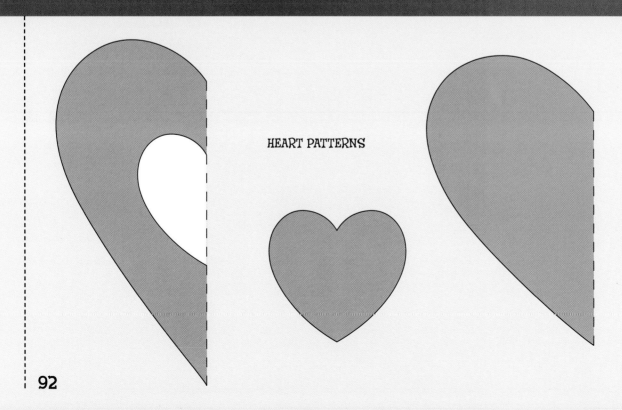

HEART PATTERNS

blooming valentine pots

what you'll need

Small flowerpot
Pink crafts paint
Paintbrush
Tracing paper; pencil
Red and pink paper
Scissors; marking pens
Pipe cleaners
Stapler and staples
Tape; fishbowl rocks or
    packages of colored
    stones (find them at
    crafts stores)

here's how

1 Paint the flowerpot with crafts paint. Let the paint dry.

2 Trace the patterns you like, left, onto tracing paper. Fold the red and pink papers in half, and trace around the half-heart pattern by placing the dotted line edge of the pattern on the fold of the paper. Cut out the hearts.

3 Write a message on each heart. Form a heart shape with the pipe cleaners, leaving a long stem.

4 Staple each pipe cleaner and paper heart together.

5 If needed, put a piece of tape over the hole in the bottom of the pot. Pour the rocks into the pot. Arrange the hearts and pipe cleaners in the pot.

what you'll need

Hard-boiled or blown-out white or brown eggs

Egg-dyeing kit or food coloring

Small round colored stickers and/or colored reinforcements (find them with office supplies at discount and office supply stores)

here's how

1 Dye the white eggs following the dye company's instructions, or mix 1 tablespoon food coloring with 1 cup of water. Drop eggs carefully into colored water and let soak for about 10 minutes. Take the eggs out of the water. Let dry.

2 Decide how you want to put the stickers on the eggs. Make polka dots, faces, flowers, or whatever you like on the colored or brown eggs.

Polka-dot eggs

The fun goes on after the dipping and dyeing is done. Make patterns on your Easter eggs using colorful stickers!

KID TESTED

Pretty Egg, by Danelle, age 4

Easter egg coasters

With dozens of colors to choose from, crafting foam is the perfect material to make coasters at Easter time.

what You'll need

Pencil; tracing paper
Scissors
Crafting foam
Thick white
    crafts glue

here's how

1 Trace the egg shape, pages 98–99. Cut out the shape. Draw around the pattern on the background color of crafting foam. Cut out the shape.

2 Using the patterns on pages 98–99 for ideas, cut shapes from foam and glue to one side of the egg. Let the glue dry.

My Crazy Eggs, by Megan, age 6

KID TESTED

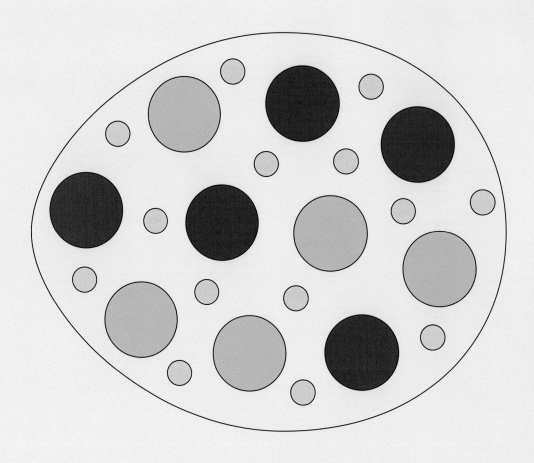

EGG PATTERNS

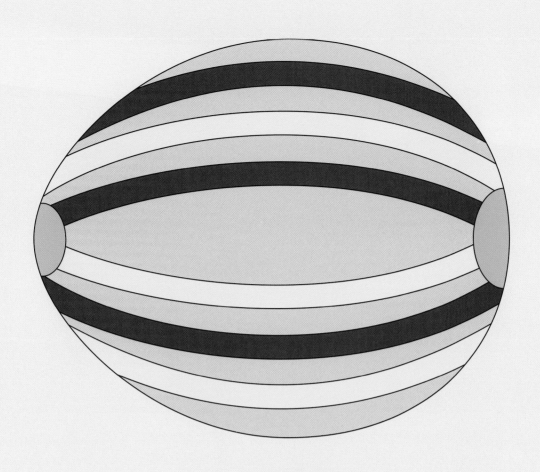

EGG PATTERNS

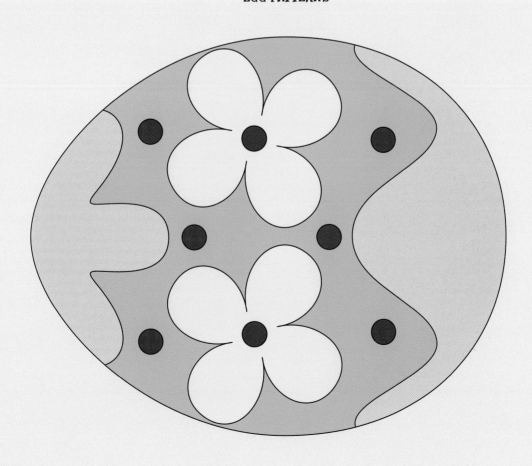

Friendship Garden, by Grace, age 7

craft with your best friend

Celebrate your "bestest" buddies with craft projects that shout friendship! You'll learn how to make an adorable pet dish, glitzy and glamorous purses, love-to-read bookmarks, rainy day umbrellas, kitty and doggy greeting cards, and a whole bunch more! So grab your best friend and craft yourselves silly!

The next time it rains, be ready with a bright umbrella you painted all by yourself!

Rainy day umbrellas

what You'll need

Sponges
Scissors
Disposable plates
Acrylic paints
Umbrella

A

you change colors. Continue adding designs with sponges until you like the way it looks. Let dry.

3 To give centers to flower designs, dip your finger in paint and press in the center of the flower. Let dry.

B

KID TESTED

Rainbrella, by Clarissa, age 5

here's how

1 Using scissors, cut sponges into several triangles or other cool shapes as shown in Photo A, above.

2 Put a small amount of each paint color on a different plate. Wet sponges with water and wring out. Dip a sponge into paint and press onto umbrella as shown in Photo B. Rinse out the sponge with water if

Bow wow-meow cards

what You'll need

Acrylic paints in gray, white, beige, brown, orange, and black

Papers in light green, blue, and pink

Toothbrush; plastic eyes

Thick white crafts glue

Black or white marking pen; scissors

5-inch-square cards and envelopes

Glue stick

Patterned scrapbook papers

here's how

1 Squeeze a quarter-size drop of paint into the center of the colored paper. Using a toothbrush and light brushing motions, spread the paint into a large animal head shape. Scrubbing the toothbrush too hard will ruin the paper. Squeeze a dime-size drop of paint on each side of the head for the ears. Brush the paint up for upright ears and down for floppy ears. Let the paint dry.

2 Use crafts glue to attach the plastic eyes and a foam triangle nose to the painting. Let the glue dry. Draw a mouth and whiskers using a black or white marking pen.

3 Trim the finished pet painting to fit on the front of the card. If you like, use glue stick to attach the pet cutout to a piece of scrapbook paper before gluing it to the card.

Cleo and Max, by Andrea and Morgan, both age 4

KID TESTED

These cute cards are
as much fun to make as they are to send to
a special friend! Just spread out a little paint using a
toothbrush to shape a furry kitty or playful puppy.

When you get together with your best friends to
play dress-up, be sure you have a special purse
for the occasion. These purses
dazzle with glitter and gems of all sorts.

Pretty purses

what You'll need

Purse (can be an old
   purse from Mom
   or Grandma)
Glitter paint
Paintbrush; jewels
Strand or loose sequins

here's how

1 Using the photos for ideas, choose how you want your purse to look. Fill in simple solid shapes, make irregular lines, follow the lines of texture that may be on the purse, or make up your own pattern. Paint on glitter paint as desired. If filling in solid areas, spread the paint with a paintbrush.

2 To add sequins or jewels, press them in the glitter paint while it is wet. Let dry.

Penny Purse, by Meredith, age 7

107

Adorable dish

what You'll need

Pet food dish

Enamel paints in colors you like

Paintbrushes

Alphabet stickers (find at scrapbook stores)

here's how

1 Using the photos, opposite and below, for ideas, paint the rim and the side of the dish. To avoid paint getting in your pet's food, leave the inside of the dish unpainted. Paint stripes, flowers, dots, or other small designs.

To paint dots, dip the handle of a paintbrush into paint and dot onto the surface. Make flower petals using a small paintbrush. To paint stripes, use a flat paintbrush. Let dry.

2 If you like, outline some of the designs with black paint. Let dry.

3 Add alphabet stickers to the side of the dish to spell a name. Press the stickers into place in a straight or wavy line.

KID TESTED

Twitcher

My Dog Dish, by Morgan, age 4

Create something special for your best animal friend—
a painted food dish with his or her name on it!

Buddy bookmarks

what you'll need

Colorful papers
Ruler
Scissors
Glue stick
Photo of friend
Paper punch
Eyelet and eyelet tool
Plastic lacing
Alphabet beads
Stitched appliqués
Thick white
  crafts glue

here's how

1 From one colored paper cut a piece $1^1/_2 \times 4$ inches for the top layer. Trim one short end into a V.

2 Using a glue stick, glue the cut paper piece on top of the background paper. Trim the background paper to be $^1/_4$ inch more than the edge of the top paper.

3 Trim a photo to measure $1^3/_4 \times 2$ inches. Glue the photo onto white paper. Trim just past the edge of the photo. Glue it to the center of bookmark.

4 Use a paper punch to make a hole in the middle of the V. Ask an adult to put an eyelet in the hole.

5 Cut a 14-inch length of lacing. Fold it in half. Push the fold through the eyelet. Bring the lace ends through the loop and pull to secure. Thread beads on each lace tail. Knot at the ends.

6 Use crafts glue to glue appliqués in place. Let the glue dry.

Make a bookmark for your best friend and put a favorite picture on it!

Rainbow Tree and Cave, by Finn, age 6

use your big imagination

Discover oodles of fantastic projects that will be different every time you make them. Paint a flowerpot doll or a bug-eyed snake planter. Shape some clay beads to make into a pretty bracelet. Print some writing paper and send a note to Grandma or a favorite friend. Learn plenty of ways to use your imagination when you make these oh-so-cool crafts!

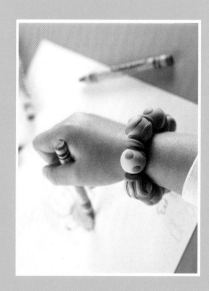

Pasta pencil holder

what You'll need

Container, such as a small oatmeal container
Acrylic paints in white, blue, green, yellow, orange,
   pink, and purple; paintbrush
Pasta in a bunch of different shapes
Thick white crafts glue; disposable plate

here's how

1 Choose a container that is clean and dry. Paint the container white or another solid color. Let it dry.

2 To cover the container, sort the pasta (see Photo A, right). Glue pasta in rows, as shown in Photo B, to create patterns around the container. Or make objects, such as the flower on the lid, opposite. Put a large dot of glue onto a plate and let it sit to thicken. Dip each piece of pasta into glue and stick it on the side of the container. Let dry.

3 Paint the covered container white. Let it dry. Paint sections using different colors as shown in Photos C and D. Let dry.

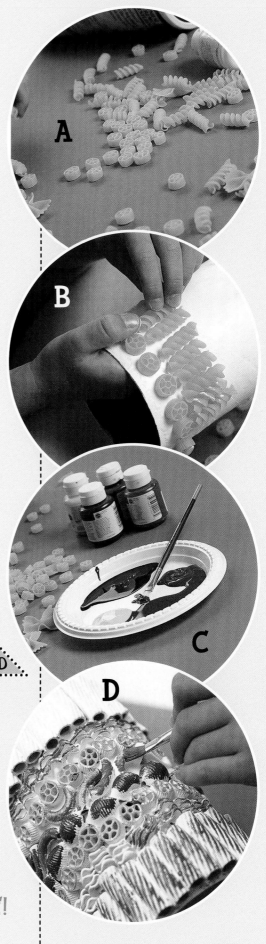

KID TESTED

Noodle Box, by Kourtni, age 8

Twisty, curvy, wavy, crazy noodles cover any box with bumpy fun. Add a stroke or two of paint, and presto—you'll have a cool place to stash your stuff!

types of pasta

SHELLS (CANNELLONI)

MOSTACCIOLI

CAMPANELLE

BOW TIES (FARFALLE)

WAGON WHEELS

RINGS (ANELLI)

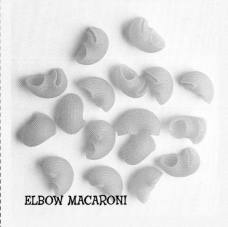

ELBOW MACARONI

PENNE

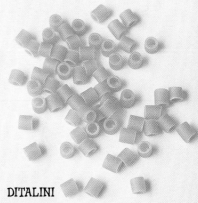

DITALINI

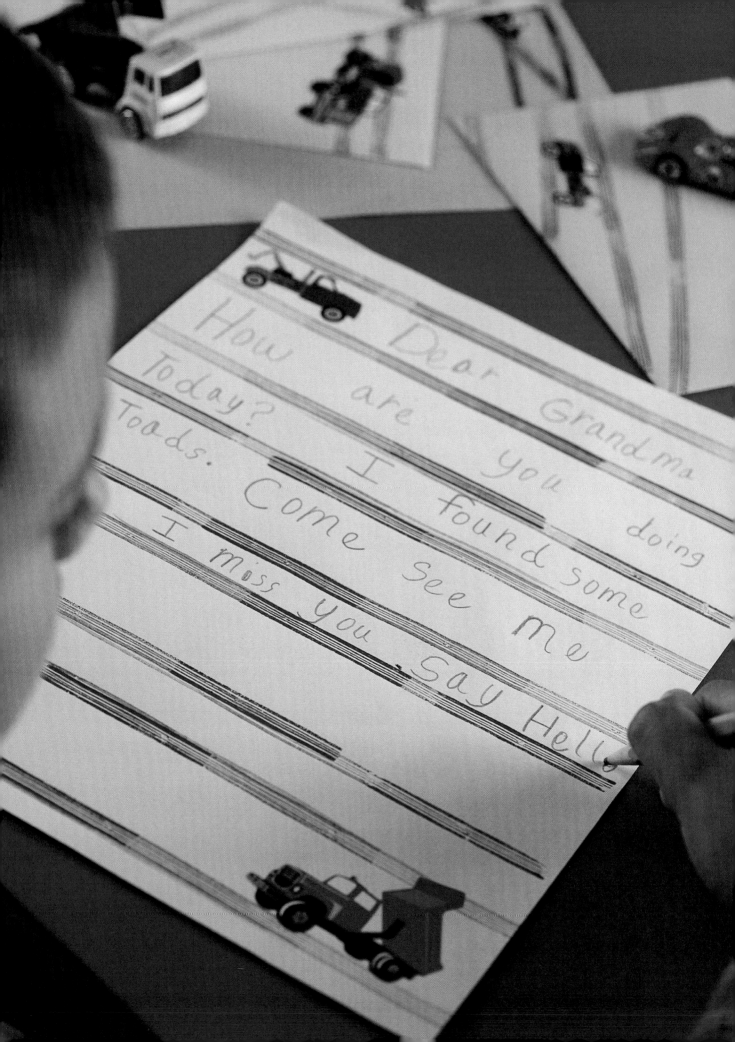

Tire tracks stationery

what you'll need

Miniature toy car with treaded wheels

Black ink pad

Colored papers and envelopes

Truck and car stickers

here's how

1 Roll the wheels of the toy car over the ink pad. Now roll them onto the papers and envelopes to leave tire tracks. Repeat this as many times as you wish, leaving room to write between the marks.

2 Place car or truck stickers over tracks. Let the ink dry.

Making notepaper is a blast with this simple stamp-and-roll technique! Hot rod, truck, and car stickers race across the one-of-a-kind stationery.

Busy bugs

You'll welcome these fuzzy flies and friends creeping along your hand or buzzing in your ear!

what You'll need

Pom-poms
Thick white
  crafts glue
Pipe cleaners
Small wiggly eyes
Quilting thread
Silver thread
Rhinestones

here's how

1 To make a dragonfly, glue five small red pom-poms together. Using the photo, above, as a guide, shape a set of wings from pipe cleaners. Use one pipe cleaner for each wing and twist the ends together in the center. Glue the wings to the underside of dragonfly body. Glue two wiggly eyes to the head. Thread a piece of quilting thread through the

head to form the antennae. If you like, tie silver thread around each body section.

2 To make the spider, cut black pipe cleaners into four 3$\frac{1}{2}$-inch pieces. Bend each pipe cleaner piece in half. Using four black pom-poms, sandwich a pair of legs between two pom-poms. Glue in place. Do this again for a second set of legs. Glue the two sections together. Glue two eyes to the head and three gold

rhinestones to the back. Bend the legs into M shapes.

3 To make the caterpillar, cut green pipe cleaners into four 3$\frac{1}{2}$-inch pieces. Bend each pipe cleaner piece in half. Form the body with five pom-poms and glue a pipe cleaner between the pom-poms. Bend the ends of each pipe cleaner to form feet. Glue eyes on the head and thread a piece of quilting thread through head to form antennae.

USE YOUR IMAGINATION!

What kind of bugs do you see where you live? Here are some ideas for more animals you can make using the same supplies:
⇒ Ladybugs
⇒ Bees
⇒ Ants
⇒ Frogs
⇒ Lizards
⇒ Snails
⇒ Fireflies
⇒ Beetles
⇒ Grasshoppers
⇒ Flies
⇒ Butterflies
⇒ Moths
⇒ Snakes
⇒ Dogs
⇒ Cats
⇒ Bears
⇒ Birds
⇒ Penguins
⇒ Owls
⇒ Monkeys
⇒ Elephants

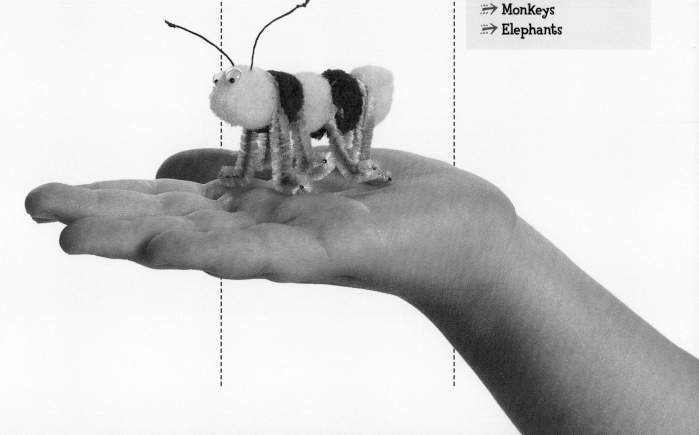

Your drawings make super patterns for creating foam works of art! Use a different drawing to make a special place mat for each person in your family.

what You'll need

One of your drawings or paintings
Tracing paper; pencil
Scissors
Crafting foam in colors you like

Artwork place mat

here's how

1 Use a drawing or painting that is as big as a place mat for a pattern. Trace the main shapes on tracing paper. Cut out the shapes.

2 Trace around the shapes on matching colors of crafting foam. Cut out the shapes.

3 Choose a large sheet of foam for the background. Glue the foam cutouts in place. Let the glue dry.

4 Use stickers, a marking pen, or paint to make any small words or letters you want on the place mat.

Thick white crafts glue Alphabet stickers, permanent marking pen, or tube-style paint

KID TESTED

Slitherin' flowerpots

what You'll need

Clear, flat glass marbles
Acrylic paints
Paintbrushes
Pencil
Terra-cotta flowerpots
Paint markers
Thick white crafts glue

KID TESTED

Silly Worm, by Danelle, age 4

here's how

1 To make the snake eyes, paint the flat sides of two marbles with dark lines down the center and white lines on both sides. Let the paint dry.

2 Using a pencil, sketch the snake's head and tongue along the rim of the flowerpot. Draw the snake's body wrapped around the pot, ending with a tail at the base.

3 Fill in the area between the pencil lines with paint, but leave several dots or stripes unpainted along the length of the snake's body to paint with a second color. Let the paint dry. Use a different color and a small paintbrush to finish by making small spots or stripes. Outline the head and any areas you like using paint markers.

4 Glue the eyes to the snake's head on the pot's rim. Let dry.

Coil these painted bug-eyed snakes around your plants for a hissing good time.

Pickup pocket

what you'll need

2 plastic-coated plates, any color
Scissors
Paper punch
Ruler
Pencil
1 long, colorful shoestring
1 pipe cleaner
Small beads
Alphabet and decorative stickers

here's how

1 Ask a grown-up to cut one plate in half, making a curved cut.

2 Punch holes along the edge of the half plate in sets of two. Make one hole 1 inch away from the other hole and then start the next set of two $1/2$ inch away.

3 Lay the half plate over the second plate and mark position of holes onto this plate. Take off the half plate and punch holes in second plate.

4 With rims facing, lace the plates together. Loop ends of shoestring around the first and last holes. Weave extra shoestring through the lacing on back of plate.

5 Punch two holes, 2 inches apart, at the center top of the whole plate. Bend a pipe cleaner in half to make a loop. Thread on a few beads if you wish. Push the pipe cleaner ends through holes to the front. String a bead on one end. Push both ends through opposite holes. Twist the ends together behind the plate.

6 Use alphabet stickers to spell "My Stuff." Put on other stickers as you wish.

Tote your treasures around the house with these helpful paper plate pockets.

A pretty painting of the outdoors creates a happy home for a shiny caterpillar made out of marbles!

what You'll need

8×10 primed studio canvas (find at art stores); pencil
Acrylic paints in sky blue, green, and other colors you like

Silly caterpillar

here's how

1 The line that separates the sky from the ground is called the horizon. Have a grown-up help draw a pencil horizon line across the canvas just below the center.

2 Paint the sky blue and the grass green. Paint the sides of the canvas too. Let the paint dry.

3 Paint flowers across the grass. Add a sun, trees, bushes, or other outdoor shapes. Let the paint dry.

4 To shape the caterpillar, arrange 11 or 12 marbles in a wavy line (like a W) on the canvas. Glue the marbles in place. Let dry.

5 Paint white eyes and spots on the marbles. To make the spots, dip a paintbrush handle into paint and dot onto the surface. Paint a black or red nose. Let dry.

6 Use a black marking pen to make antennae, legs, and a dot in the center of each eye. Place the painting on an easel.

Paintbrush
Green flat marbles
Thick white crafts glue
Glass paints in white, black, red, and other colors you like
Black permanent marking pen; easel

KID TESTED

Morgan's Bug, by Morgan, age 4

Rev up your engine, and decorate a storage bin that's perfect for keeping toy cars and trucks together.

what You'll need
Laminated foil sheet, such as Reynolds craft foil, or heavy-duty foil
Pad of paper or stiffened felt
Assorted round lids

Toy car caddy

here's how

1 Turn over the foil sheet on a cushioned work surface, such as a pad of paper or stiffened felt. Put two lids along the bottom of the foil sheet. To draw the car wheels, use a dull pencil to trace around the lids.

2 Connect the wheels with one line to make the bottom of the car. Draw the front, top, and back of the car with one line that curves up from one wheel and down to the other. Add windows, door handles, lights, exhaust pipes, and other wanted car parts. Trace over the lines a second time to make sure you can see the drawing well on the other side.

3 Flip the foil over and fill dented-in areas with paint. Let dry. Flip the drawing over and fold under $1/2$ inch of foil on every side.

4 Tape the foil piece to paper. Trim the paper, leaving a border. Tape it to the other paper. Trim it and tape it to a piece of foam. Trim the edges even. Tape it to the container.

Dull pencil; paintbrush
Slick paint or acrylic
    paint in red, yellow,
    blue, and black
Double-stick tape
2 patterned papers
Scissors; crafting foam
Plastic storage
    container

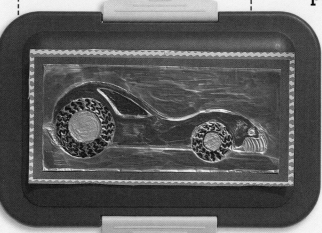

Use your memory to make one of these nifty dolls look like you or one of your friends. These flowerpot pals keep you company hanging on a curtain rod, bedpost, or bookshelf.

Ryan Lucas, by Ryan, age 8

KID TESTED

what you'll need

1½-inch wood bead for head; paintbrush
Acrylic paints
Cotton swab
Black fine-tip marking pen
Small terra-cotta flowerpot
White chalk; drill
2 crafts sticks; string
Clear acrylic spray
Heavy metal washer
Thick white crafts glue
2 pieces of cord, each 22 inches long

here's how

1 Paint bead a face color. Let dry. Paint the hair. Use a cotton swab to apply watery red paint for cheeks. Let dry. Use the pattern, right, as a guide to draw eyes and a mouth with a marking pen.

2 Turn pot upside down and use chalk to draw arms and clothes designs on pot.

3 Paint the clothes and arms on the pot. Let dry. Outline the details with a marking pen.

4 Ask a grown-up to drill a small hole ½ inch from one end of each crafts stick. Paint sticks to look like stockings and shoes.

5 Ask a grown-up to spray pot, doll head, and crafts sticks with acrylic spray in a work area outside or one with open windows.

6 Thread string through holes in top of legs and tie each leg to the washer. Apply glue to the knots of the string.

7 Place the two 22-inch-long cords side by side; fold them

in half. Loop the cords around the top of the washer. Tie a knot 1 inch above the washer.

8 Thread cord through hole in pot, pulling knot up to inside of pot's bottom. Tie another knot on the outside of the pot next to the hole.

9 Thread cords through hole in the bead head and tie a knot at top of head. Knot the ends of the cords together to form a hanging loop.

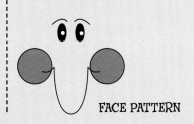

FACE PATTERN

132

Bangle bracelet

what You'll need

Oven-bake clay, such as Sculpey; waxed paper Small straw; baking dish Scissors; heavy elastic string; ruler

here's how

1 To make a round bead, pinch off a marble-size piece from clay. Roll into a ball. To twist colors, pinch off a pea-size piece from a different color of clay. Roll the clay into a thin snake shape. Wrap the snake piece around the ball, pressing into place. To make polka dots, pinch off tiny pieces of clay. Roll each piece into a ball. Press onto the larger clay ball.

2 To make a flat bead, pinch off a pea-size piece of clay. Flatten with palm of hand on a piece of waxed paper.

3 To make a hole in each bead, press a straw through the center and remove.

4 Place the clay beads on a baking dish. Ask a grown-up to bake the clay pieces in the oven following the package directions. Let cool.

5 Cut a piece of elastic 5 inches larger than your wrist. String beads on elastic until only about 4 inches of the elastic is left. Knot the elastic ends together. Trim the ends of the elastic.

KID TESTED

Beautiful Bracelet, by Morgan, age 4

Oven-bake clay comes in so many colors. Pick your favorites to make awesome beads to wear around your wrist or to share with a friend.

Go ahead–flap your arms and squawk like a bird! When you wear this crazy cap, you can act as looney as you like!

Birdy cap

what you'll need

Tracing paper; pencil
Scissors
Crafting foam in
    yellow, white,
    and black
Thick white crafts
    glue
Heavy book
Baseball cap
Bobby pins
Large colored feather
Tape
Ball to fit in cap

here's how

1 Trace the patterns, pages 138–139, onto tracing paper. Cut out the patterns and trace onto foam. Cut out the foam shapes.

2 Using a small amount of glue, stick the black middles and eyebrows onto the white eyeballs. Change the position of the black foam pieces to make different expressions. Put the middles close together and the eyes one above the other to make the bird look cross-eyed. Place the middles in the center for a look of surprise. Move the middles to the bottom to make the bird look down or on the top to make the bird look up. Set a heavy book on the pieces until dry.

3 Glue the beak onto the bill of the hat. Use bobby pins to hold it in place while the glue dries.

4 Tape the large feather in the middle of the front of the hat.

5 Place the hat over a ball to make it easier to glue on the eyes. Glue on the eyes and tape them in place while drying. When all the glue is dry, remove the tape and ball.

KID TESTED

Cornelius Crow, by Jacob, age 7

137

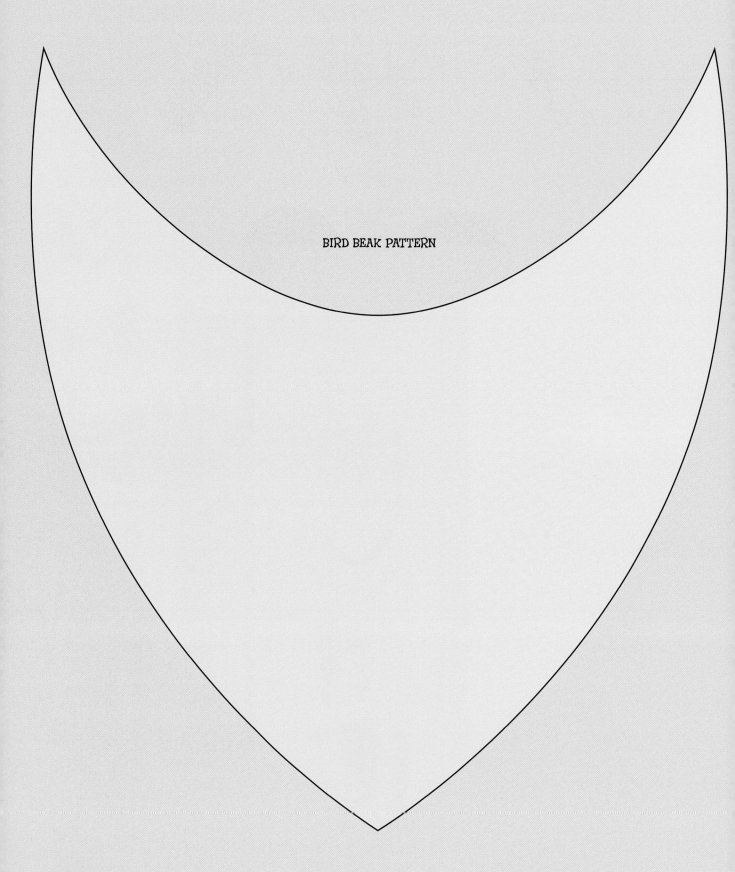

BIRD BEAK PATTERN

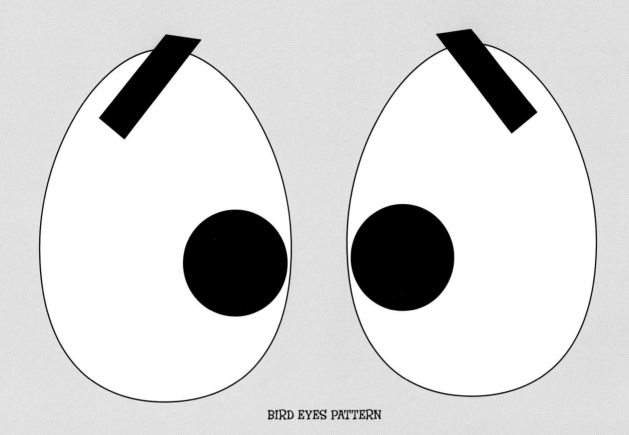

BIRD EYES PATTERN

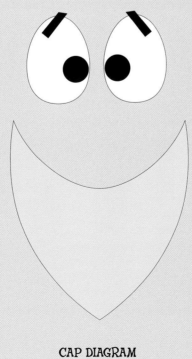

CAP DIAGRAM

Ballet bag

Design a sweet carryall that's perfect for toting your tutu and dance shoes! With just a few easy steps, create your very own ballet bag.

what you'll need

Mesh tote bag
24 hair clips
6 ball-style ponytail holders; scissors

here's how

1 Clip five hair clips between the handles on each side of the bag.

2 Cut two ponytail holders in half. Using one half, thread the ends through two holes in the center of the mesh bag. Knot the ends on the inside of the bag. Tie on the three other cut ponytail holder halves close to the first one. Wrap a whole ponytail holder around those tied to the bag. Clip seven hair clips around the ponytail holders.

3 Turn over the bag and repeat Step 2.

Credits

Crayon drawing artists

Finn Hoogensen
Jacob Hoogensen
Laurel Hoogensen
Grace Ann Peelen
Olivia Claire Peelen

Designers

Susan M. Banker
Heidi Boyd
Carol Dahlstrom
Phyllis Dunstan
Alice Wetzel

Kid-tested artists

Morgan Banker
Ryan Banker
Danelle Bramow
Andrea DuVall
Michaela King
Olivia King
Jacob Lundeen
Erica Matsuyama
Yuuki Matsuyama

Tess Nygren
Evelyn Ochs
Meredith Quinlan
Con Robinson
Kourtni Robinson
Clarissa Tusa
Jack Tusa
Lindsay Wright
Megan Wright

Models

Eva Ames
Lisa Ames
Rylee Ames
Jonathan Bailey
Lauren Bailey
Morgan Banker
Danelle Bramow
Nicole Bramow
Erin Bundt
Courtney Carlson
Drew Carlson
Andrea DuVall
Tierra Fletcher
Conner Heckart
Laurel Hoogensen
Jonas King
Michaela King
Olivia King
Warren King
MacKenzie Mathis
Erica Matsuyama

Yuuki Matsuyama
Tess Nygren
Evelyn Ochs
Maureen Ochs
Palmer Ochs
Keegan Shay
Madison Steffen
Patrick Steffen
Clarissa Tusa
Jack Tusa
Emma Wetzel
Andrew Wright
Lindsay Wright
Megan Wright

Photography

Andy Lyons
   Cameraworks
Peter Krumhardt
Scott Little

Photostyling

Carol Dahlstrom
Donna Chesnut,
   assistant

index

If you enjoyed this book, look for these other inspiring titles for KIDS!

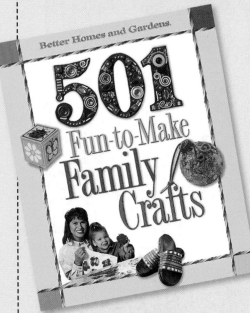

No matter what the season, now you can enjoy gathering together as a family to express your creativity! This big book of crafts offers
* More than 500 "fun-tastic" ideas
* 224 project-packed pages
* Dozens of great patterns
* Holiday projects, nature crafts, jewelry making, and more!

This book for kids ages 6-14 will bring out your child's creative spirit! All 45 projects are kid tested, so you know your child will love making:
* Cool paper crafts
* Neat stuff to wear
* Cute dolls and puppets
* Nifty painted projects
* Great gifts for all seasons

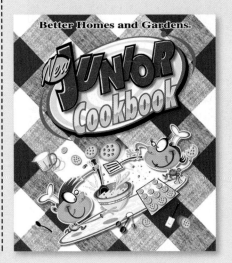

Your kids will love mealtime when they're kings and queens of the kitchen! This ringbound book includes more than 50 kid-tasted, kid-tested, kid-approved recipes for yummies, such as Doubly Crusty Pizza, Tangled Twisters, and Riddle Griddle Bread—PLUS easy-to-follow instructions, nutritional information, and all the basics every young cook needs to know!